PIP AND BUNNY: PIP AT THE SEASIDE

The invaluable 'Pip and Bunny' collection is a set of six picture books with an accompanying handbook and e-resources carefully written and illustrated to support the development of visual and literary skills. By inspiring conversation and imagination, the books promote emotional and social literacy in the young reader.

Designed for use within the early years setting or at home, each story explores different areas of social and emotional development. The full set includes:

- six beautifully illustrated picture books with text and vocabulary for each
- a handbook designed to guide the adult in using the books effectively
- 'Talking Points' relating to the child's own world
- 'What's the Word?' picture pages to be photocopied, downloaded or printed for language development
- detailed suggestions as to how to link with other EYFS areas of learning.

The set is designed to be used in both individual and group settings. It will be a valuable resource for teachers, SENCOs (preschool and reception), Early Years Staff (nursery, preschool and reception), EOTAs, Educational Psychologists, Counsellors and Speech Therapists.

Maureen Glynn has 25 years' experience teaching primary and secondary age children in mainstream, home school and special school settings, in the UK and Ireland.

First published 2020
by Routledge
2 Park Square, Milton Park, Abingdon, Oxon OX14 4RN

and by Routledge
52 Vanderbilt Avenue, New York, NY 10017

Routledge is an imprint of the Taylor & Francis Group, an informa business

British Library Cataloguing-in-Publication Data
A catalogue record for this book is available from the British Library

Library of Congress Cataloging-in-Publication Data
A catalog record for this book has been requested

ISBN: 978-0-367-19104-7 (pbk)
ISBN: 978-0-429-35496-0 (ebk)

Typeset in Calibri
by Apex CoVantage, LLC

Visit www.Routledge.com/9780367136642

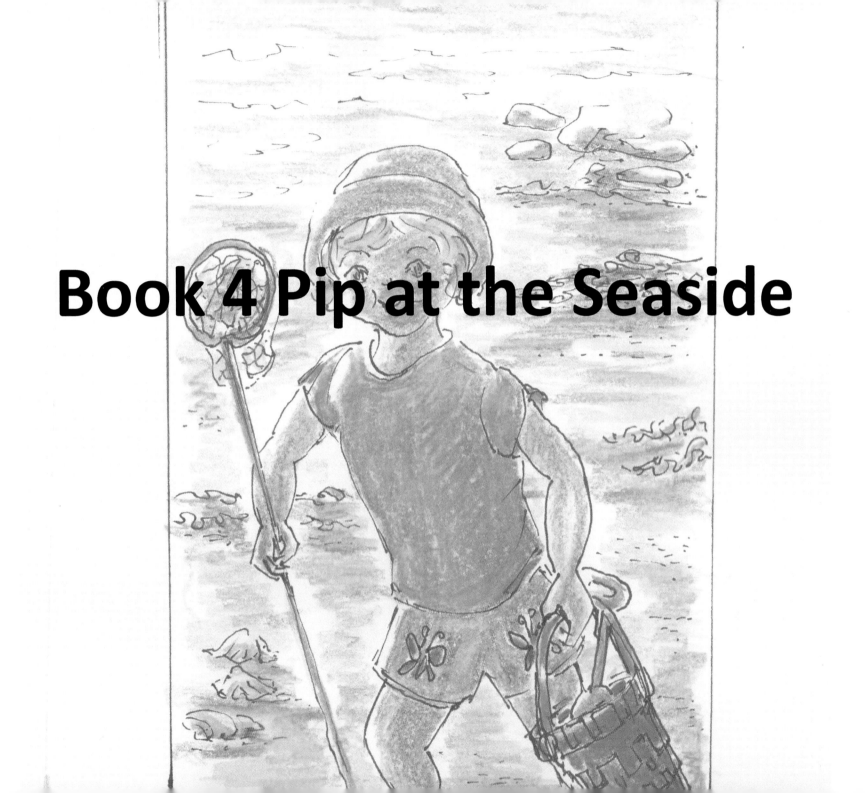

Book 4 Pip at the Seaside

One sunny day in Summer, Pip and Bunny visit Nanna and Grandad who live near the sea.

Pip's cousins, Joey and Anna, live close by too.

Joey wants to show Pip and Bunny his favourite place to explore, when the tide is out.

They run across the rocks and kneel to look into the clear pools of water. They see spikey sea urchins, barnacles, shrimps, baby crabs and, under some seaweed, a beautiful, vivid, orangey-red starfish with seven arms!

While Bunny takes a nap, Pip, Joey and Anna build a splendid castle made of sand.
Daddy puts a flag on the tall central tower and makes arrow slits in the turrets around the edge.

The cousins put on armbands to go paddling in the sea.
They have fun splashing each other.

Then they fetch their buckets to fill with water and...

pour it into the moat surrounding the sandcastle. 'It looks like a real castle now!' says Pip.

But suddenly, an excited puppy comes running towards them...

The puppy can't stop… Oh dear!

He lands right on top of the castle and slowly sinks into the sand.

Everyone laughs because he looks so funny.
But Pip is cross and starts to cry.

She hugs Bunny and Daddy consoles her.
Mummy and Aunt Lucy buy ice-lollies for everyone.
Pip cheers up and laughs at the puppy too.

The children get dressed and look for sea-shells to collect on the seashore.
They find...

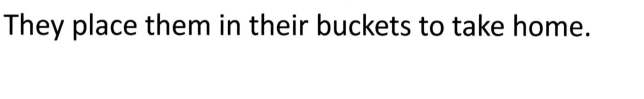

Limpets, cockles, blue mussels, pearly oysters and tiny periwinkles.
Pip loves their different shapes and colours.
They place them in their buckets to take home.

They have fun drawing faces in the sand, using their spades and fingers to make the lines.

Back with Nanna and Grandad, Pip, Joey and Anna can't wait to tell them about their exciting day.

Then everyone enjoys fish and chips, sitting around the kitchen table.

Book 4 Pip at the Seaside What's the Word?

Show the page and ask the child to say words that explain each image:

Page 17 Action Words?

Page 18 Location Words?

Page 19 Descriptive Words?

Page 20 Seaside Words?

Page 21 Emotions and Feelings?

Action Words?

Location Words?

Descriptive Words?

Seaside Words?

Emotions and Feelings?